23 recipes from the witch's cauldron

The
Room
on the
Broom
Cookbook

Based on the picture book by

Julia Donaldson • Axel Scheffler

MACMILLAN CHILDREN'S BOOKS

Contents

Witch and Chips and Other Meals

Shortbread Stars and Other Sweet Treats

How to Use This Book: Guidelines for Grown-Ups

This book is all about having fun with food. It's perfect for introducing young *Room on the Broom* fans to cooking and is full of great ideas for everyday meals, special treats and party snacks to share with family and friends.

Every step-by-step recipe has been specially designed for adults and children to use together. The instructions are for adults to follow, but there are stages in each recipe that are an ideal opportunity to get a child involved – look out for the JOIN IN! star.

The steps in the recipe that aren't marked with a JOIN IN! star may be unsafe or complicated for a child, so it's recommended that you do those yourself. Keep a close eye on children in the kitchen at all times, and be especially careful of anything hot or sharp.

All oven temperatures are based on a fan oven, so you'll need to add about 20°C if you have a conventional oven.

You'll see a Tips, Tricks and Twists section on most pages, where you can find helpful hints and possible alternatives to try, so have fun and experiment!

Before you get started, read the hints and tips on the next page with your child.

Hints and Tips to Read Together

Are you ready to make lots of tasty treats from the witch's cauldron? Here are a few hints and tips to help you get started.

- Remember to wash your hands so they're nice and clean. Cooking can get messy, so put on an apron and tie your hair back if it's long.

- Before you start, read the recipe together so you can make sure you have everything you need. You might find it helpful to weigh, measure or count out your ingredients so they are ready to use.

- Always wash fruit and vegetables before you cook or eat them.

- Be careful of anything hot – remember things that have just come out of the oven or off the hob will take a while to cool down, so don't touch. Ouch!

- Sharp knives are for grown-ups only.

- Lots of these recipes will ask you to mix, squash or shape using your hands. Make sure you wash them before and afterwards, especially if you've used raw meat or egg.

- Not all uncooked ingredients or mixtures are safe to eat, so check with a grown-up first.

- You can get stuck in and help every time you see the JOIN IN! star, so keep your eyes open, roll your sleeves up and get ready to have some fun!

Breakfasts

Fruity Frogs

Full Moon Pancakes

Eggy Owls

Magic Potion

As Green As Can Be Omelette

Blow-away Bows

Fruity Frogs

"I am a frog, as clean as can be.
Is there room on the broom for a frog like me?"

Makes
6
frogs

You will need:

1 large green apple
2 tablespoons
  peanut butter
2 strawberries
12 blueberries
18 grapes

A sharp knife
A butter knife

What to do:

1 Cut the apple into twelve thin wedges and carefully remove the core from each slice.

2 Cut three thin slices from the middle of each strawberry for the frogs' tongues.

JOIN IN! 3 Lay the apple slices on a chopping board with the green skin pointing towards you.

JOIN IN! 4 Using a butter knife, gently spread a little peanut butter on the top of each slice.

JOIN IN! 5 Lay a strawberry slice on top of the peanut butter on six of your apple slices, then put a slice of apple on top of each one, with the peanut butter facing down.

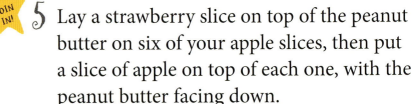

6 Now you need to make some eyes! Cut the base off twelve of your grapes.

JOIN IN! 7 Balance two grapes on top of each of your apple frogs. You could stick these in place with a small blob of peanut butter.

JOIN IN! 8 Put a blueberry on top of each grape as a pupil. You can use peanut butter to stick these in place, too.

9 Cut your remaining six grapes in half lengthways and use a small, sharp knife to cut each half into a froggy foot shape.

JOIN IN! 10 Place two feet in front of each frog. Now they're ready to eat!

Tips, Tricks and Twists

🍃 Why not put your frogs on some cucumber lily pads? Thinly slice a cucumber and then cut a little triangle out of each slice to make a lily pad shape.

🍃 If you don't want to use peanut butter, you could use a small amount of cream cheese instead.

Full Moon Pancakes

These savoury pancakes are great
for breakfast or lunch!

Makes
6
Pancakes

You will need:

200g plain flour
400ml milk
2 large eggs
A knob of butter
6 slices of cheese

A sieve
A large mixing bowl
A medium frying
  pan
A small circle cutter
A big circle cutter
A whisk
A ladle
A spatula
A measuring jug
A saucer

What to do:

 1 Break the eggs into a saucer and pick out any pieces of shell.

 2 Sift the flour into a large bowl and make a well in the centre.

 3 Pour in the milk and eggs, whisk until you have a smooth batter then set aside.

 4 Using your circle cutters, cut out small and large circles of cheese and set aside.

5 Place the pan on the heat and add a knob of butter. Once it has melted, add a sixth of the batter and spread it around the pan.

6 When the pancake is nearly cooked through, place a few cheese circles on the top then flip it over and cook the other side for about 1 minute.

7 Put the first finished pancake on a plate, and continue with the rest of the mixture.

Leave to cool before you tuck in!

Tips, Tricks and Twists

🍃 Red Leicester works well as the cheese in this recipe, as your moon craters will show up really well.

🍃 Don't worry if you don't have circle cutters – bottle tops and jar lids work just as well for cutting out the cheese circles!

🍃 If you want to serve a batch of pancakes all together, put a heatproof plate in the oven on a low heat and add your pancakes to it until you've used all your mixture.

Eggy Owls

Make your own eggy owl for breakfast!

Makes
2
owls

You will need:

2 eggs
2 stuffed green olives
1 carrot
Small bunch of basil
 leaves
1 tablespoon cream
 cheese or mayonnaise
1 piece of bread

A small saucepan
A small bowl
A small circle cutter
 (or bottle lid)

What to do:

1 Place your eggs in the saucepan and add enough cold water to cover them.

2 Put the pan on the heat. When the water starts to boil, set your timer for 8 minutes.

3 When the time is up, transfer the eggs to a bowl of cold water and leave to cool.

 4 Once the eggs are cool, tap them on a hard surface and carefully peel off the shell.

 5 Give the eggs a quick rinse to remove any stubborn bits of shell, then set aside.

6 Peel and then cut the carrot into four thin rounds. Use a sharp knife to cut away small triangles to make your owls' clawed feet. You can use two of these triangles as noses!

7 Cut two thin slices from each of your stuffed olives to make four eyes.

8 Cut the top third off your eggs.

9 Add a dollop of cream cheese to the flat part of the eggs, then stick your eyes and the carrot nose onto the cream cheese before putting the top of each egg back on. Stick two basil-leaf wings on either side of each egg with cream cheese.

10 Toast your piece of bread, then butter it and cut it into two strips – these are the branches for your owl to perch on.

11 Use a circle cutter or bottle top to make a hole in each strip of toast then place an owl into each hole.

12 Place two carrot feet just in front of each owl and then add some basil leaves to the end of your tree branches.

Tips, Tricks and Twists

If you want your owl to be a bit squidgy in the middle, let the water boil for 6 minutes before you take it out. You could make some extra tree branches to dip into the yolk if you do this.

It might be helpful to put your egg in an egg cup while you add its features.

He looks too good to eat!

Magic Potions

Iggety, ziggety, zaggety, ZOOM!

Make your own delicious magic potions.

Fruity Forest

Makes 2 Potions

You will need:

8 blackberries

5 raspberries

2 strawberries

½ banana

A splash of milk

1 tablespoon yoghurt

A food processor

JOIN IN!

What to do:

1 Count out your berries into a bowl.

2 Add the berries, banana, yoghurt and milk to the food processor and whizz it up for about 20 seconds or until it looks smooth enough to drink. If it looks too thick, add a splash more milk and whizz it for a few more seconds, then pour it into your glasses.

Magical Mango

Makes 2 Potions

You will need:

½ mango

½ banana

½ pear

1 tablespoon yoghurt

A food processor

What to do:

1 Add the mango, banana, yoghurt and pear to the food processor then whizz it up for about 20 seconds until it turns yellow and smooth.

2 When you are happy with the consistency, pour it into your glasses.

Make a wand to stir your magic potion with:

You will need:

A slice of mango
A handful of any of these
    fruits, or a mixture:
    blueberries
    red and green grapes
    strawberries
    raspberries

A kebab stick or
a narrow straw

What to do:

JOIN IN! 1 Take your kebab stick or straw and slide your fruit onto it in any order you want.

JOIN IN! 2 Use a star cutter to cut a fruit star from your mango slice. Slide it onto the top of your wand.

Tips, Tricks and Twists

🌿 You can use any fruit you want to make your potion or your wand. You could try apple, melon, pineapple or kiwi – just ask a grown-up to cut it into chunks for you first.

🌿 Why not layer your smoothie so it's yellow AND purple?

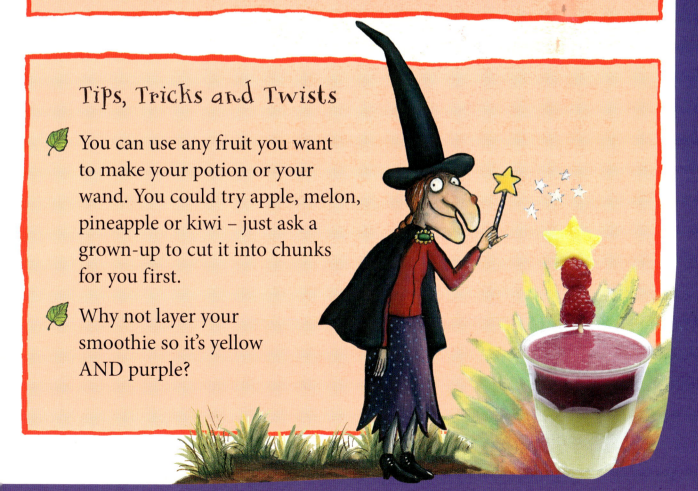

As Green As Can Be Omelette

"I am a bird, as green as can be.
Is there room on the broom for a bird like me?"

Makes
1
omelette

You will need:

50g baby spinach
Small handful of
   chives
40ml milk
2 eggs
A knob of butter
Half a cucumber
1 teaspoon cream
   cheese
1 black olive
A small slice of cheese

A small bowl
A medium-sized bowl
A frying pan, about
   20cm diameter
Safety scissors

What to do:

 1 Using safety scissors, cut up the chives and half the spinach as finely as you can.

 2 Break the eggs into the small bowl and pick out any pieces of shell.

 3 Put the eggs, spinach and chives into the medium-sized bowl, then add the milk.

 4 Mix with a fork until all the egg yolks have broken and the mixture is looking green.

5 Melt the butter in a pan over a low heat. Tip the egg mixture in and cook for about 8 minutes until set, then flip the top of the omelette over for the bird's wing.

6 Slide the omelette out of the pan and onto a plate. Leave to cool while you get the decorations ready.

7 Take the cucumber and cut two round slices and two sticks, each stick about 5cm long. Then cut two triangles from one of your round slices. These are the bird's head, legs and tail.

8 Chop the olive in half for your bird's eye and cut the slice of cheese into a triangular beak shape.

Yum

JOIN IN!

9 Take the round cucumber slice. This is your bird's head. Put a little dollop of cream cheese on it and add half an olive on top for his eye.

JOIN IN!

10 Now decorate your omelette: add the head, tail and beak, two cucumber sticks for legs and spinach leaves as feathers. You can copy the picture below.

Tips, Tricks and Twists

🍃 There are lots of green ingredients you could you use instead of chives. You could try parsley, cress, dill, or even pesto.

🍃 If you're really hungry, you could sprinkle some grated cheese on top.

Blow-away Bows

. . . away blew the bow from her long ginger plait!

Makes **8** bows

You will need:

1 sheet ready-made
  puff pastry (350g)
8 teaspoons raspberry
  jam
1 egg
Butter for greasing

A baking tray
A butter knife
A sharp knife
A small bowl
A pastry brush

What to do:

1 Preheat the oven to 200°C/Gas Mark 6.

JOIN IN! 2 Dip a piece of kitchen roll in butter and rub it all over the baking tray.

JOIN IN! 3 Lay out the sheet of puff pastry with the short end towards you. Use a butter knife to cut it in half from top to bottom so you are left with two long, thin pieces.

JOIN IN! 4 Cut each of your pieces widthways into eight, so you have sixteen rectangles.

JOIN IN! 5 Spread a teaspoon of raspberry jam on eight of your rectangles.

JOIN IN! 6 Carefully put a clean rectangle of pastry on top of each jam-covered one.

7   Cut each of your rectangular jam sandwiches into a bow shape. It's best to use a sharp knife for this as it can be quite fiddly.

8   Break the egg into a small bowl and pick out any pieces of shell, then mix it up with a fork until smooth.

9   Dip a pastry brush into the beaten egg and brush each of your bows with the egg mixture.

10   Bake in the oven for 15-20 minutes until golden brown.

Tips, Tricks and Twists

🍃 You could make your bows spotty, just like the witch's! Once they have cooled, decorate them with spots of jam.

🍃 If you're wondering what to do with the leftover pieces of puff pastry, why not bake them in the oven too? They may not look like bows, but they'll still be delicious.

🍃 You could try using apricot, strawberry or blackcurrant jam.

Snacks

Cauldron Rolls

Cheese Wands

Windy Day Salad

Creepy Crawly Crackers

Ginger Plait Loaf

Pinecones

Cauldron Rolls

Then she filled up her cauldron and said with a grin,
"Find something, everyone, throw something in!"

Makes
4
cauldrons

You will need:

4 small crusty rolls
1 large ripe avocado
A squeeze of lime
6 cherry tomatoes
1 carrot
1 small tin tuna
1 small tin sweetcorn
1 tablespoon Greek
  yoghurt

A sharp knife
A chopping board
2 small bowls
A spoon and a fork

What to do:

1 Chop the top off the bread rolls.

JOIN IN! 2 Gently pull out the fluffy bread in the middle of each one so you have four hollow rolls. These will be your cauldrons. You can eat the fluffy centre now.

3 Chop the avocado in half and remove the stone, then chop the lime in half.

JOIN IN! 4 Spoon the avocado out of its skin into a small bowl. Add a squeeze of lime, then mash both together with a fork.

5 Finely chop the tomatoes.

JOIN IN! 6 Add the tomatoes to the mixture and stir them in gently.

7 Empty the drained tins of tuna and sweetcorn into the other small bowl.

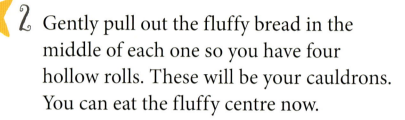

8 Add a tablespoon of yoghurt and stir the mixture together.

 9 Put the empty cauldrons onto serving plates, then fill two with the avocado mixture and two with the tuna mixture.

10 Cut four thin strips of carrot, about 10cm long. They need to be thin enough that they can be bent into cauldron handles!

11 Take each of your cauldrons and poke either end of the carrot strip into the mixture to create a handle.

Tips, Tricks and Twists

- You could add anything you want to these cauldrons. How about houmous and grated carrot? You could even fill it with baked beans, but you'd probably need a spoon to eat them with! Coriander or chives make great toppings.

- You could make the handle out of cucumber, if you'd rather.

Cheese Wands

They shot through the sky to the back of beyond.
The witch clutched her bow but let go of her wand.

Makes **12** wands

You will need:

120g plain flour
50g butter (cubed)
50g cheddar (grated)
1 small egg (beaten)
Extra flour for dusting
Extra butter for
  greasing

A baking tray
A large mixing bowl
A small star-shaped
  cutter
A pastry brush
A rolling pin

What to do:

1 Preheat the oven to 180°C/Gas Mark 4.

JOIN IN! 2 Dip a piece of kitchen roll in butter and rub it all over the baking tray.

JOIN IN! 3 Add the flour and butter to the bowl and rub together with your fingers until the mixture is like crumbly breadcrumbs.

JOIN IN! 4 Add the grated cheddar and mix.

JOIN IN! 5 Stir in ¾ of the beaten egg and use your hands to shape the mixture into a ball. Pull off ¼ of the dough and set aside.

6 Sprinkle some flour on a clean surface and roll out the big ball of pastry. Aim for a rectangle that's 25cm long and 12cm wide, with the short edge facing you.

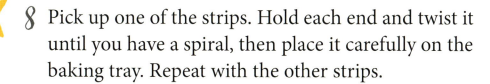

7 Cut your rectangle widthways into twelve strips.

JOIN IN! 8 Pick up one of the strips. Hold each end and twist it until you have a spiral, then place it carefully on the baking tray. Repeat with the other strips.

9 Now roll out the smaller ball of pastry. It should be the same thickness as the strips.

JOIN IN! 10 Press the star cutter into the pastry to make 12 stars.

JOIN IN! 11 Brush a little of the leftover beaten egg onto the end of each strip and press a star down on top. Brush a little beaten egg all over each wand.

12 Bake in the oven for about 15 minutes or until golden brown.

Tips, Tricks and Twists

🍃 If you don't have lots of time, you could use ready-made pastry and sprinkle cheese over the top before cutting into strips. Make sure you keep aside some pastry for the stars, though.

🍃 You might need to bake your wands in two batches, depending on how big your baking tray is.

Windy Day Salad

This delicious salad is great fun to make and to eat!

Makes 2 salads

You will need:

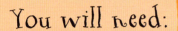

6 big handfuls of
   salad leaves
1 large carrot
1 yellow pepper
1 handful of dried
   pasta bows
1 teaspoon runny
   honey
1 tablespoon white
   wine vinegar
2 tablespoons olive oil

A large saucepan
A sharp knife
A chopping board
A star-shaped cutter
A small saucepan
A clean jam jar

What to do:

1 Boil a saucepan of water and cook the pasta according to the instructions on the packet. Drain and set aside.

2 Remove the stalk and seeds from the pepper and cut it into quarters. Lay them out on the chopping board.

JOIN IN!
3 Press the star cutter into the pepper to make eight stars

4 Peel the carrot and cut it in half. Then cut each half into long thin slices and lay them out on the chopping board.

5 Cut your carrot slices into hat shapes.

JOIN IN!
6 Spread three big handfuls of salad leaves on each plate.

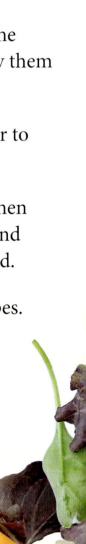

7 Arrange the carrot hats, pepper stars and pasta bows on top.

 8 Now make your dressing. Put the honey, oil and vinegar in the jam jar.

 9 Put the lid on the jam jar and give it a really good shake.

10 Using a teaspoon, drizzle some dressing over your salads.

Tips, Tricks and Twists

You could make witch's hats out of cucumber slices instead.

If you don't have a star cutter, you could cut star shapes out of the yellow pepper using a sharp knife.

Creepy Crawly Crackers

These crackers are great fun
to make with friends.

Makes LOTS of bugs!

You will need:

A packet of plain
  biscuits or crackers
Smooth peanut butter
Cream cheese
A few chives
Fruit and vegetables:
  carrots
  grapes
  raspberries
  cucumber
  strawberries
  red pepper

A big tray
Safety scissors
A sharp knife
A butter knife

What to do:

1 Cut up the fruit and vegetables and lay
them out on a big tray. It works well to
have rounds of carrot, halved grapes,
rounds of cucumber cut in half and
slices of strawberry.

JOIN IN! 2 Spread peanut butter or cream cheese on
a biscuit with your butter knife.

JOIN IN! 3 Turn it into a bug using fruit and
vegetables! Be as creative as you want –
have a look at these for ideas.

You could use chocolate chips for eyes

Try a bug made of raspberry and blackberry

How about a butterfly made with four round carrot wings and a thin strip of pepper for a body?

Tips, Tricks and Twists

🌿 You could use safety scissors to cut chives to the right length, but if you want smaller chunks of other ingredients, ask a grown-up to chop them up for you.

🌿 The bits of fruit you might usually pick off, such as the leafy part of the strawberry or the stem of the grape, can make great hats or antennae for your creepy crawlies. Just remember to remove these before you eat your bugs!

🌿 You can use any fruit, vegetable or herb you like. Why not see what you've got in the fridge?

Chives make great antennae!

Ginger Plait Loaf

The witch had a cat and a very tall hat,
And long ginger hair which she wore in a plait.

Makes
1
large loaf

You will need:

500g strong white
  flour
1 teaspoon salt
1 teaspoon sugar
2 teaspoons yeast
1 tablespoon olive oil
350ml warm water
60g Red Leicester
  cheese (grated)
Extra flour for dusting
Extra oil for greasing
1 egg (beaten)

A large mixing bowl
A baking tray
A clean surface for
  kneading
A pastry brush

What to do:

 1 Grease your baking tray with some oil.

 2 Add the flour, salt, sugar and yeast to the large bowl, mix together and then make a well in the middle.

 3 Pour the warm water and oil into the well and stir the mixture to make a rough ball.

 4 Sprinkle some flour on a clean surface, then place the ball of dough in the middle.

 5 Knead for 5-10 minutes, until the dough is smooth, not sticky. If the dough feels too wet, add more flour a teaspoon at a time.

6 Put the dough on the baking tray and cover with a tea towel. Leave it in a warm spot for about an hour to rise.

 7 Once it has risen, knead in the cheese. Then divide the dough into three pieces, and roll each piece into a 40cm long strand.

 8 Place the strands side by side on the baking tray, leaving about a 3cm gap between them.

 9 Pinch the three strands together firmly at the top end of the tray, then tuck the end under.

10 Plait the dough! Lift the strand on the right and pass it over the centre strand. Take the strand on the left and pass it over the centre strand. Continue plaiting the dough by placing the right strand over the centre strand, then the left strand over the centre strand, keeping the plait nice and tight.

11 When you've plaited all the way to the bottom, pinch the ends together and tuck them under. Cover the plait with a tea towel and leave it in a warm place for an hour.

12 Preheat the oven to 180°C/Gas Mark 4. Brush the plait with beaten egg, and bake for 20 minutes.

13 Check to see if the plait is cooked by tapping the bottom. If it sounds hollow, it's cooked. If not, give it 5 more minutes and check again.

Kneading is tiring work— try taking it in turns!

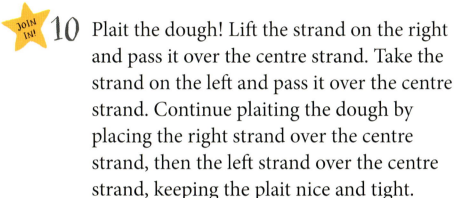

Pinecones

The cat found a cone . . .
These tasty pinecones make a great snack.

Makes
24
pinecones

You will need:

100g oats
60g dried apricots
1 tablespoon honey
2 tablespoons
   peanut butter
3 tablespoons water

Sprinkles for coating:
   oats
   cocoa powder
   linseeds
   pumpkin seeds

A food processor
A large mixing bowl
4 small plates

What to do:

1 Put the oats, water, apricots, honey and peanut butter into the food processor. Whizz together to make a sticky mixture. Add another dash of water if the mix doesn't feel very sticky.

2 Transfer the mixture into the bowl, then put it in the fridge for a few minutes.

3 Sprinkle each of your coatings onto separate plates. You might have a plate with cocoa powder, a plate with oats, a plate with linseeds and a plate with pumpkin seeds.

This is great fun to do with your friends

4 Take the large bowl with the mixture in it out of the fridge.

 5 With clean hands, take a small chunk of mixture and roll it to make a bite-sized ball.

 6 Roll the ball in one of your coatings, then set to one side.

 7 Repeat this with the rest of the mixture until you have a lovely pile of pinecones!

Tips, Tricks and Twists

🍃 You can try these with all sorts of other ingredients. You could add chopped nuts, dates, or even chocolate chips.

🍃 If you want your pinecones to look snow-covered, you could roll them in desiccated coconut.

🍃 They'll last for two weeks in an airtight container.

I like the look of the chocolate-covered ones!

Meals

Fiery Dragon Pasta

Witch and Chips

Bog Balls

Roasted Dragon

As Keen As Can Be Pizza

Fiery Dragon Pasta

Don't worry – this pasta may look red and fiery but
it's not spicy enough to make you breathe fire!

Makes 3 helpings

You will need:

500g cherry tomatoes
1 teaspoon olive oil
6 slices of chorizo
  or salami
180g pasta
Half a ball of
  mozzarella
3 black olives

A large mixing bowl
A baking tray
A large saucepan
Safety scissors

What to do:

1 Preheat the oven to 180°C/Gas Mark 4.

 2 In the large bowl, mix the tomatoes and oil with your hands.

3 Tip the tomatoes onto the baking tray then roast in the oven for 15 minutes and leave to cool.

 4 Cut the chorizo into little pieces using a pair of safety scissors.

 5 Once cool, put the tomatoes back into the large bowl and squash them with your hands into a lumpy sauce.

6 Stir in the chorizo pieces.

7 Cut the mozzarella into six circles and nine triangles. Halve the olives.

8 Fill a large saucepan with boiling water and cook the pasta according to the instructions on the packet.

9 Drain the pasta and add it to the mixing bowl with the sauce. Mix until your pasta is fiery and red.

10 Transfer to serving bowls.

11 Add some eyes and teeth as a finishing touch: put three triangles of mozzarella in a line, and two circles above. Now add half a black olive to each circle of mozzarella.

Tips, Tricks and Twists

- This recipe makes three child-size helpings, or two adult portions.

- If you want a sauce that is less fiery, you could use salami or ham instead of chorizo.

- You could add lots of other things to your pasta. Why not try chopped-up red pepper, fresh herbs, sweetcorn or a handful of spinach?

Witch and Chips

These hat-shaped fishcakes go really well
with the courgette chips on page 40!

with the courgette chips on page 40!

Makes
6
hats

You will need:

250g potatoes
A knob of butter
2 fillets of fish
   (about 250g)
500ml milk
Zest of 1 lemon
2 eggs
100g breadcrumbs
Olive oil
Extra butter for
   greasing

A large saucepan
A large mixing bowl
A potato masher
A medium-sized
   saucepan
A slotted spoon
A baking tray
2 shallow bowls

To make your witch hats:

1 Peel and chop the potatoes into chunks.

2 Bring a large saucepan of water to the boil
   and add the potatoes. Cook until soft.

3 Drain the potatoes and put them in the
   large mixing bowl.

JOIN IN!

4 Add a knob of butter and mash the
   potatoes until there are no lumps left.

5 Put the fish in a medium-sized saucepan
   and pour in enough milk to cover.

6 Gently heat until the milk starts to bubble,
   then simmer the fish for 8-10 minutes
   until cooked through.

7 Remove the fish from the milk using
   a slotted spoon and set aside to cool.

8   Dip a piece of kitchen roll in butter and grease the baking tray.

9   Preheat the oven to 180°C/Gas Mark 4.

 10   When the fish is cool, flake it into little pieces and add to the mashed potato with the lemon zest. Mix it all up. You can use your hands but make sure you wash them first.

 11   Divide the mixture into six roughly even balls and shape each ball into a triangular hat shape. Put them to one side.

 12   Break the eggs into one of the shallow bowls and pick out any pieces of shell. Mix the eggs well with a fork.

13   Put the breadcrumbs in the other shallow bowl.

 14   Now for the really messy bit! Carefully dip one of your hats in the egg mixture until it is covered.

 15   Put the eggy hat in the bowl of breadcrumbs until it is completely covered. Repeat with all six hats and put them onto the baking tray.

 16   Drizzle with olive oil and bake for 15-20 minutes.

Now turn the page and make your chips.

Witch and Chips

"I'm planning to have WITCH AND CHIPS for my tea!"

You will need:

3 courgettes
1 teaspoon dried
  herbs
½ teaspoon salt
½ teaspoon pepper
1 tablespoon olive oil
Extra oil for greasing

A large mixing bowl
A baking tray
A small bowl

Makes 3 helpings

To make your chips:

1 Preheat the oven to 180°C/Gas Mark 4.

JOIN IN! 2 Dip a piece of kitchen roll in olive oil and rub it all over the baking tray.

3 Cut the ends off the courgettes and discard.

4 Chop the courgettes into thirds, and then cut each third into wedges. Put the wedges in the large mixing bowl.

JOIN IN! 5 Put the dried herbs, salt and pepper in the small bowl and mix well with a spoon.

JOIN IN! 6 Add the tablespoon of oil to the herb mix and mix again.

JOIN IN! 7 Tip the mixture over the courgette wedges. Get every last bit out of the small bowl.

8 Give everything a really good mix so the wedges are evenly covered. It's best to use your hands!

 9 Put the coated wedges on the baking tray and spread them out evenly.

10 Bake in the oven for 15-20 minutes.

Tips, Tricks and Twists

- Don't eat any of the raw fishcake mix as it can make you ill.

- You can use any fish you like, but white fish such as cod or haddock is best. If you want to speed things up, you could use tinned tuna or salmon.

- You could use potato, sweet potato or butternut squash for your chips. These will need longer in the oven though.

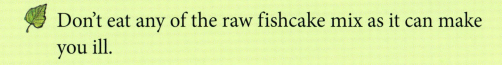

Bog Balls

These meatballs taste much nicer than anything you might find in a bog.

Makes 15 balls

You will need:

500g beef mince
1 small red onion
2 tablespoons breadcrumbs
1 teaspoon mixed dried herbs
1 egg
Olive oil for greasing
250ml passata (tomato sauce)
A handful of basil leaves
Parmesan cheese (grated)

A baking tray
A large mixing bowl
A big saucepan
Safety scissors

What to do:

1 Preheat the oven to 200°C/Gas Mark 6.

 2 Dip a piece of kitchen roll in olive oil and rub it all over the baking tray.

3 Tip the mince into the large mixing bowl.

4 Finely chop the onion.

 5 Break the egg into a small bowl and pick out any pieces of shell. Now use a fork to beat it until it is a smooth yellow mixture.

6 Add the onion, dried herbs, breadcrumbs and egg to the mince.

 7 Now it's time to get messy! Wash your hands, then use them to mix all the ingredients together, making sure everything is really well combined.

Don't eat any of the raw mixture

8 Take a small handful of the mixture and squash it into a ball. Put the meatball on the baking tray, rolling it around so it is evenly covered in oil.

 9 Repeat until you have used up all your mixture. You should have 12-15 meatballs. Don't forget to wash your hands afterwards!

10 Cook in the oven for 20 minutes.

 11 Cut up the basil leaves using safety scissors.

12 Heat the passata in a big saucepan over a low heat, then add the basil and the cooked meatballs. Simmer for a few minutes, then put in bowls to serve, sprinkling with a little parmesan cheese.

Tips, Tricks and Twists

🍃 It's especially important to wash your hands before and after handling raw meat.

🍃 You don't have to use beef mince – you could use pork, lamb or vegetarian mince instead.

Roasted Dragon

"I am a dragon, as mean as can be . . ."

Makes 2 dragons

You will need:

1 large red pepper

50g couscous (uncooked)

1 carrot

1 tablespoon sweetcorn

4 pumpkin seeds

¼ courgette, chopped into pieces

3 cherry tomatoes, chopped into chunks

A few leaves of basil (chopped)

Greaseproof paper

A baking tray

A medium mixing bowl

A heatproof bowl

Safety scissors

A peeler

What to do:

1 Preheat the oven to 180°C/Gas 4 and line a baking tin with greaseproof paper.

2 Put the couscous in a heatproof bowl and cover with boiling water. Leave for 10 minutes or until the couscous is cooked.

3 Cut your carrot in half. Chop one half into small pieces, and use a peeler to make thin ribbons from the rest.

4 Once the couscous has cooled, place it in the mixing bowl.

 JOIN IN!

5 Mix in the chopped carrot, courgette, tomatoes, basil and sweetcorn, setting aside 4 grains of sweetcorn for later.

6 Chop the top of the pepper off, but don't throw it away. Get rid of the pepper seeds then cut the pepper in half lengthways and lay both halves skin-side up on the greaseproof paper.

That looks so real

7 Push the couscous into each pepper half.

8 Bake both peppers in the oven for 20 minutes.

 9 While the peppers are cooking, take the leftover pepper top and use safety scissors to cut some ears.

10 Once the filled pepper halves are cooked and cooled, transfer them to a plate.

 11 Add your dragon's ears, pumpkin-seed nostrils and sweetcorn eyes. Cut your carrot ribbons into flame shapes with safety scissors and place by his mouth.

Tips, Tricks and Twists

Why not sprinkle some feta in with your couscous mixture too?

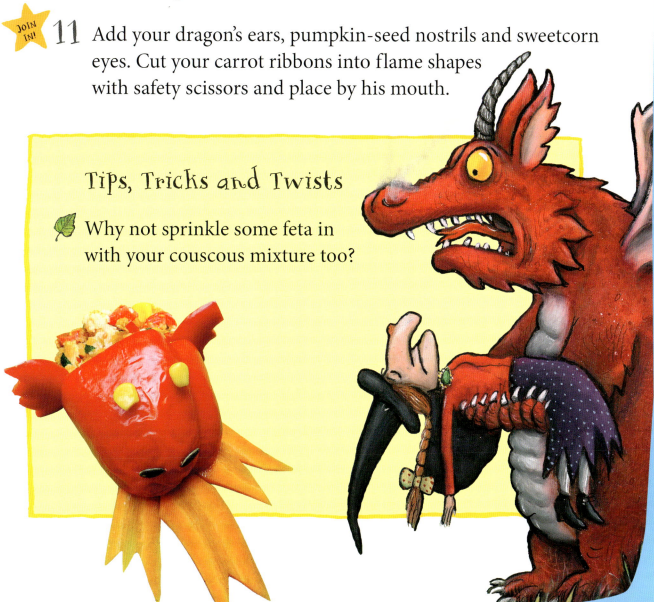

As Keen As Can Be Pizza

Make your own mini pizzas, then decorate them to look just like dogs.

Makes **8** Pizzas

You will need:

200g flour
2 teaspoons baking powder
A pinch of salt
1 teaspoon dried herbs
1 tablespoon olive oil
100ml warm water
8 tablespoons tomato sauce
60g cheese (grated)
2 slices of salami
8 black olives
Half a red pepper
Extra olive oil for greasing
1 ball of mozzarella

A baking tray
A large mixing bowl
A rolling pin
A circle cutter (10cm)

What to do:

1 Preheat the oven to 220°C/Gas Mark 7.

 2 Dip a piece of kitchen roll in a little olive oil and grease the baking tray.

 3 Put the flour, baking powder, salt and herbs in the large mixing bowl and stir.

 4 Make a well in the middle and add the oil. Pour in the water a little at a time and mix until you have a soft dough.

 5 Use your hands to squash the dough into a ball and knead it for a minute or two.

 6 Sprinkle a little flour on a clean surface and roll out the dough until it's ½ cm thick.

 7 Use the circle cutter to press eight circles out of the dough then lay them on the baking tray, not too close together.

8   Prepare your decorations: cut each salami slice into eight wedges. Cut each olive into two thin rounds for eyes and one big piece for a nose. Slice the mozzarella into eight, and make eight thin curved slices from the pepper.

9   Spread a tablespoon of tomato sauce on each pizza then add a sprinkling of cheese and two salami ears.

10 Cook in the oven for 10-12 minutes then let cool slightly.

11 On each pizza, add a circle of mozzarella for the muzzle, a slice of pepper for a mouth and finish off with olive slices for eyes and a shiny black nose!

Tips, Tricks and Twists

If you don't like olives, you could use sweetcorn for eyes and a cherry tomato as a nose.

It's best to cook your pizzas in two batches as they expand when cooking. Make sure you place them at least 5cm apart on the baking tray.

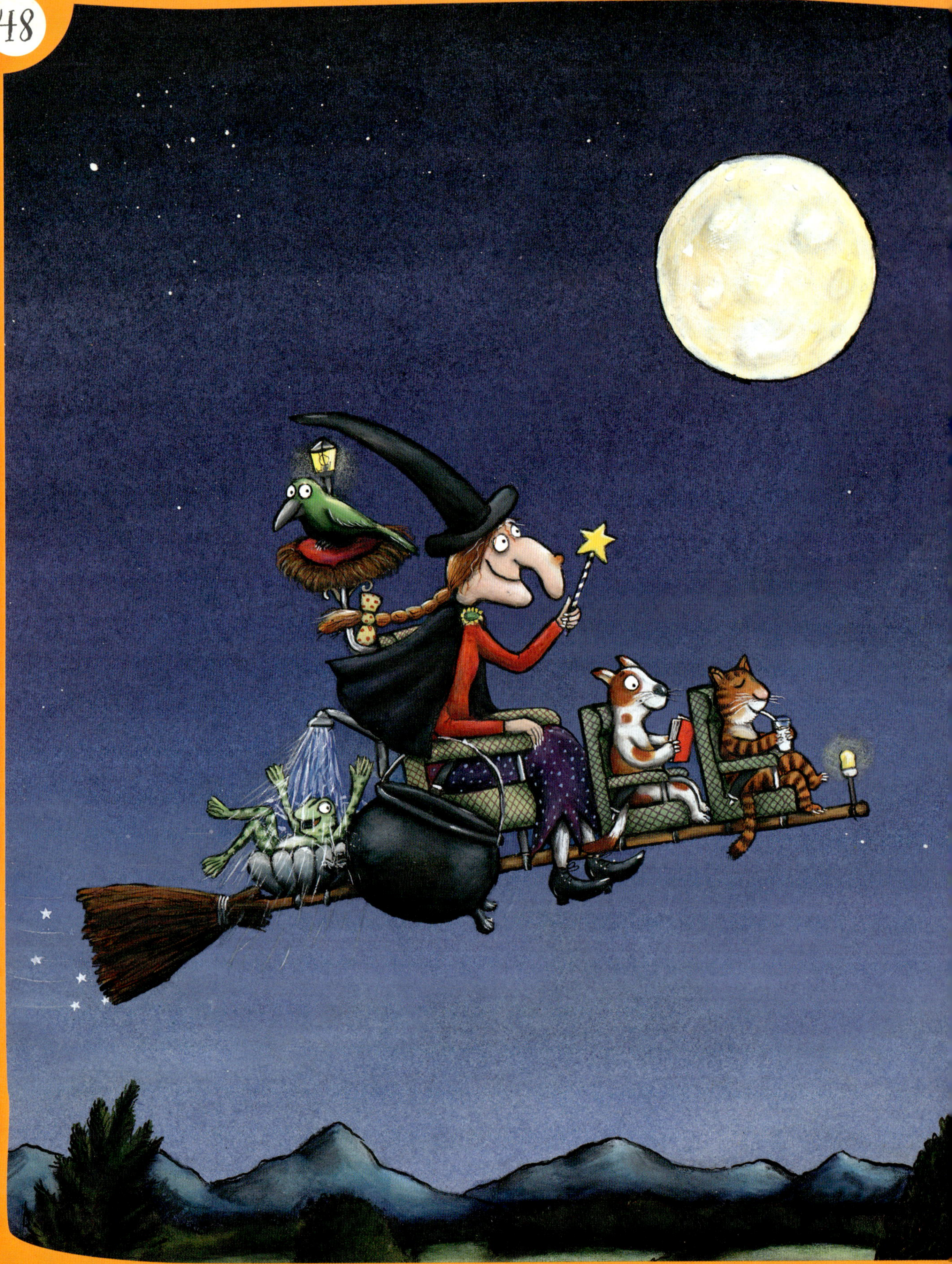

Sweet Treats

Purple Pudding

Birds' Nests

Tasty Toadstools

Shortbread Stars

Horrible Beast Cake

Purple Pudding

These rice pudding pots make a delicious dessert.

Makes 4 helpings

You will need:

100g pudding rice
600ml milk
8 teaspoons sugar
12 ripe raspberries
8 ripe blackberries
Butter for greasing
Handful of leftover
   berries for decoration

Four ramekins,
   8cm diameter
A sieve
A clean sandwich bag
A baking tray

What to do:

1 Preheat the oven to 160°C/Gas Mark 3.

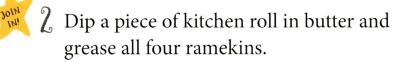 2 Dip a piece of kitchen roll in butter and grease all four ramekins.

3 Put the rice in a sieve and give it a really good wash under running water.

4 When all the water has drained, divide the rice evenly between the ramekins.

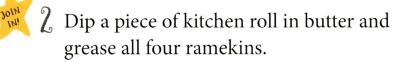 5 Add two teaspoons of sugar to each ramekin and mix it with the rice.

6 Put the raspberries and blackberries in a clean sandwich bag and seal it tightly shut. Try not to trap any air inside.

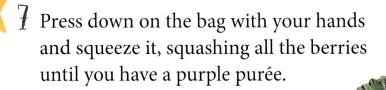 7 Press down on the bag with your hands and squeeze it, squashing all the berries until you have a purple purée.

8 Spoon out the purple purée, dividing it equally between the four ramekins, then stir it in.

9 Add 150ml of milk to each ramekin and gently stir it in.

10 Put the four ramekins on a baking tray and cook in the oven for 60-75 minutes.

11 Wait for the ramekins to cool, then add a few berries for decoration and tuck in!

Tips, Tricks and Twists

- You can tell when your rice pudding is cooked because it will wobble slightly when you shake it.

- Why not try this with different fruit? You could use ripe strawberries, peaches or blueberries.

- If you want to make a rice pudding that's less sweet, you could halve the amount of sugar or try using honey instead.

Birds' Nests

The bird shrieked with glee . . .
Try making these delicious chocolate birds' nests.

Makes
12
nests

You will need:

25g unsalted butter
150g chocolate
2 tablespoons honey
90g shredded wheat
Small bag of blanched
   hazelnuts

A small saucepan
A big bowl
12 paper cases
A muffin tray

What to do:

JOIN IN! 1 Break the chocolate into pieces with your hands and put into the small saucepan. Add the butter and honey.

2 Melt over a low heat. Stir until everything is combined and leave to cool.

JOIN IN! 3 In your big bowl, crumble the shredded wheat with your fingers.

4 Pour the chocolate mixture in your saucepan over the shredded wheat.

JOIN IN! 5 Mix everything together so the shredded wheat is totally coated in chocolate.

JOIN IN! 6 Put the 12 paper cases into the muffin tray.

JOIN IN! 7 Divide the mixture between the paper cases. Use a big spoon to scoop it out of the bowl, and then scrape the mixture into the paper cases using a teaspoon.

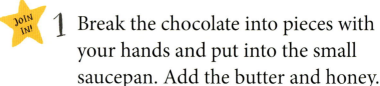

8 With the teaspoon, make a little well in the middle of each nest. You could use clean fingers for this, but it will be messy!

9 Place three hazelnuts into each nest – for the birds' eggs.

10 Put in the fridge for two hours to set.

Tips, Tricks and Twists

🌿 If you want to make these nests even more of a treat, you could use chocolate eggs instead of hazelnuts.

🌿 If you're feeling creative, why not try and make a bird out of green fondant icing to perch on top of the eggs?

🌿 You could add raisins or chopped nuts to the mixture, too!

Tasty Toadstools

Squash some raspberries to make these toadstool ice creams.

Makes 4 toadstools

You will need:

150g natural yoghurt
12 raspberries
Handful of white
   chocolate chips
1 tablespoon
   raspberry jam

A medium-sized
   mixing bowl
4 empty yoghurt pots
   (individual sized)
4 lolly sticks
A small bowl

What to do:

JOIN IN! **1** Count the raspberries out into the mixing bowl, then squash them with your hands until they look like raspberry juice.

JOIN IN! **2** Wash your hands, then add the yoghurt and jam to the raspberries and mix it all together so the yoghurt turns dark pink.

JOIN IN! **3** Set the yoghurt aside and take your empty yoghurt pots. Place a few white chocolate chips at the bottom of the pot. These will be the toadstools' spots.

JOIN IN! **4** Blob a spoon of yoghurt into the pot, then put a few more chocolate chips around the side. Then fill up the rest of the pot.

5 Place the pots in the freezer. After an hour, take them out and slide a lolly stick into the middle of each pot.

6 Put the pots back in the freezer for another hour, or until the yoghurt feels frozen all the way through.

7 Fill your bowl with warm water. After taking the pots out of the freezer, dip them in the water for a few seconds to loosen the frozen yoghurt.

 8 Take hold of the lolly stick and gently pull out your toadstool. Eat it quickly before it melts!

Tips, Tricks and Twists

🍃 If you don't have any yoghurt pots, you could use small cupcake cases. You just have to make sure the mixture is deep enough to slide a lolly stick into.

🍃 You could use any red berries to make your yoghurt go pinky-red. You could even use strawberry yoghurt.

You should never eat real toadstools – they can be poisonous!

Shortbread Stars

Make some scrumptious stars with this easy shortbread recipe.

Makes about 24 stars

You will need:

180g plain flour

120g butter, softened and cut into cubes

1 teaspoon vanilla extract

60g caster sugar

Extra flour for dusting

Extra butter for greasing

A sieve

A baking tray

A large mixing bowl

A star-shaped biscuit cutter

A rolling pin

What to do:

1 Preheat the oven to 180°C/Gas Mark 4.

JOIN IN! 2 Dip a piece of kitchen roll in butter and rub it all over the baking tray.

JOIN IN! 3 Sift the flour into the mixing bowl. Add the butter and rub together with your fingers until the mixture resembles breadcrumbs.

JOIN IN! 4 Add the vanilla extract and sugar, and mix together. Then squeeze the dough into a ball with your hands.

5 Sprinkle your work surface with flour and roll the dough out to about ½ cm thick with a rolling pin.

6 Use the biscuit cutter to cut out the stars and carefully place them on the baking tray. Re-roll any leftover dough to make more biscuits.

7 Bake the shortbread for 12-15 minutes or until they're a pale golden colour. You might need to do two batches.

Tips, Tricks and Twists

🌿 Leave a little gap between each star when you place them on the baking tray in case they spread slightly.

🌿 You could make your stars spotty by mixing some chocolate chips into the dough.

🌿 Why not shape some triangle hats out of the dough, too? You could even try a broomstick if you're feeling brave!

Horrible Beast Cake

From out of a ditch rose a horrible beast . . .
This beast takes a bit of time to create – but it's worth it!

You will need:

200g unsalted butter
200g caster sugar
5 eggs
200g plain flour
4 tablespoons cocoa
   powder
3 teaspoons baking
   powder
1 tablespoon milk
Extra butter for
   greasing

A round cake tin,
   20cm diameter
A muffin tin with at
   least four holes
A large mixing bowl
A rubber spatula
A wire rack
A food processor

Make your sponge:

1 Preheat the oven to 180˚C / Gas Mark 4.

 2 Dip a piece of kitchen roll in some butter and grease the cake tin and four holes in the muffin tin.

3 Cream the butter and sugar in the food processor until pale and fluffy. Transfer to the large mixing bowl.

 4 Break the eggs into a bowl and pick out any pieces of shell, then add the eggs and milk to the butter and sugar and mix well.

 5 Sieve the flour, baking powder and cocoa powder into the mixture and fold together.

 6 Put a large tablespoon of mixture in each hole in the muffin tin.

7 Pour the rest of the mixture into the cake tin, then put both tins in the oven. After 30 minutes, take out the muffin tin.

8 Cook the main cake for a further 15-20 minutes. Check if it's cooked by inserting a knife. It should come out clean.

9 Remove the cake and muffins from their tins and transfer to a wire rack to cool.

You will need:

300g dark chocolate
50g white chocolate
210ml double cream

A large mixing bowl
A large saucepan

Make two types of ganache:

JOIN IN!

1 Break the dark chocolate into squares and put in a large mixing bowl.

2 Pour in 180ml of double cream.

3 Place over a saucepan of boiling water on a low heat and stir until the chocolate and cream have combined and you have a glossy chocolate sauce.

4 Put to one side to cool.

5 Repeat using the white chocolate and 30ml of double cream.

Make some decorations for your bog.
You don't have to make all of these – you can pick and mix.

You will need:

1 tablespoon of dark
   chocolate ganache
1 teaspoon of white
   chocolate ganache
10 small chocolate
   biscuits
Mint leaves
1 mini marshmallow
1 raspberry
Black liquorice laces
Red strawberry laces
Green strawberry laces
White chocolate
   buttons
White chocolate drops
Green fondant icing
Yellow marzipan
1 kiwi
3 strawberries
½ mango

Cocktail sticks
A sharp knife
Flower cutters
   (different sizes)

Clean a nice big surface and lay out all your ingredients for decoration-making. Make sure you have your ganache from earlier!

Make two trees:

Stack mini chocolate biscuits on top of each other with dark ganache. Put a big blob of ganache on top of each tree and stick a bunch of mint leaves to it.

Make a toadstool:

Push a cocktail stick through a mini marshmallow so about 1cm of stick pokes up. Put a raspberry on top and dot it with white ganache using another cocktail stick.

Make a bird's wing:

Take a bit of green fondant icing and mould into a wing shape. You can press a mint leaf into it and peel it off again to give the wing a bit of texture.

Make some eyes:

Take a few white chocolate buttons and put a small blob of dark ganache on each one. To make your frog's eyes, roll out two small balls of green icing and flatten with your finger. Push a white chocolate drop into each one and add a small blob of dark ganache.

Make the cat's tail:

Roll out a long thin sausage of marzipan and tightly wrap a black liquorice lace around it.

Make some bugs:

Use any leftover ingredients to make some bugs to live in your bog. You could try and copy these ones.

Make some flowers:

Slice the kiwi, mango and strawberries. Use your flower cutters to make different-sized flowers from the fruit slices. Finish them off with a little ball of marzipan or green icing.

Make a broken broom:

Use a pair of safety scissors to cut black liquorice laces into twenty 4cm lengths. Arrange the black laces around a chocolate finger and tie in place with a red lace.

Now it's time to put everything together.
Have your cooled sponge and all your decorations at the ready.

You will need:

The sponge cake
The four muffins
The decorations
The leftover dark
    chocolate ganache
The leftover white
    chocolate ganache
30–40 chocolate
    fingers, snapped
    in half

A bread knife
Cocktail sticks

What to do:

1 When the cake is completely cold, use a bread knife to level off the top.

JOIN IN! 2 Stack up your four muffins on top of the cake. You could use cocktail sticks to fix them in place. (Remove before serving!) This is your horrible beast.

JOIN IN! 3 Stick the halved chocolate fingers all the way round the outside of the cake, using the dark ganache as glue.

JOIN IN! 4 Pour the rest of your dark chocolate all over the stacked-up muffins and the top of the cake. What a muddy bog!

If your ganache has hardened, put it in the microwave for 15 seconds before pouring.

5 Now it's time to add your decorations! Stick the trees and toadstool into the cake.

 6 Stick the eyes, cat's tail, and bird's wing into the stacked-up muffins. You've made a horrible beast!

 7 Stick your broken broom into the cake at an angle, then add half a chocolate finger for the other half.

 8 Swirl some white chocolate ganache into the muddy bog of dark ganache so it looks like muddy puddles.

 9 Stick your flowers and bugs all over the cake to finish it off.

Use ganache to stick me on!

First published 2018 by Macmillan Children's Books
an imprint of Pan Macmillan
20 New Wharf Road, London N1 9RR
Associated companies throughout the world
www.panmacmillan.com

ISBN: 978-1-5098-7628-0

1 3 5 7 9 8 6 4 2

A CIP catalogue record for this book is available from the British Library.

Printed in China